Original title:
The Magic Beneath the Tree

Author: Julian Carmichael
ISBN HARDBACK: 978-9916-94-092-1
ISBN PAPERBACK: 978-9916-94-093-8

Enchanted Roots

Once a squirrel wore a hat,
Dancing 'round, what of that?
Chasing shadows, tail in twirl,
Claiming he’d be the next big pearl.

A worm said, "I can do a jig!"
To the beat of a bouncy fig.
But wobbling too much, he fell flat,
And laughed when he saw a nearby rat.

Secrets in the Sylvan Shade

In the shade, whispers giggle,
A raccoon found a sword to wiggle.
He proclaimed, "I'm knightly now!"
Till tripping on roots made him bow.

A wise old owl gave a hoot,
'That sword's just a stick, oh what a hoot!'
The raccoon grinned, still feeling cool,
Declaring himself the court of fools.

Beneath Canopy Dreams

Beneath branches, dreams take flight,
A bumblebee dressed up so bright.
Sipping nectar, he spun ‘round,
Declaring himself the king of sound.

A butterfly joined in the chase,
Doing flips in a dizzy race.
They tumbled over leaves so green,
Chortling madly, what a scene!

The Lure of Leafy Lore

Underneath green layered tales,
A turtle shared his fishy fails.
"I tried to swim and look so slick!"
But instead, he took a chubby flick!

A grasshopper laughed with glee,
“Let’s put on a comedy spree!”
With jokes about towers of hay,
As we giggled the afternoon away.

Beneath the Old Oak's Embrace

Squirrels dance in the shade,
Chasing their tails, unafraid.
Twigs turn to swords, bark to shields,
In this kingdom, laughter yields.

With acorns as treasures, they scheme,
A world of fun, bursting at the seam.
Birds chirp jokes, I swear they're wise,
While ants hold court with tiny ties.

Nature’s Hidden Canvases

Dandelions paint the floor,
While bees snicker, craving more.
Ladybugs play peek-a-boo,
On petals dressed in morning dew.

A toad croaks out a silly song,
While butterflies glide on winds so strong.
Nature's jesters, wild and free,
Crafting giggles under the spree.

The Enigma of Twisting Vines

Vines tangled in a playful hug,
Sneaking snacks like a sly little bug.
The forest's riddle has a grin,
As raccoons dance, let the antics begin.

Twisting like thoughts in a tangled mind,
Woodpecker's drumming, the beat's so unrefined.
In this twisty land, jesters prevail,
Mischief and fun weave a hilarious tale.

Forests Breath with Secrets

Whispers float on a gentle breeze,
Trees gossip as they sway with ease.
Groundhogs chuckle from their burrows,
Sharing tales of their brave furrows.

A fox slips by with a smirk so sly,
“Who let the bees out?” he quips on the fly.
The woods erupt in bursts of glee,
So many secrets, just wait and see.

Celestial Roots

In a forest so vast, where the squirrels wear hats,
The roots do a dance, while the trees chat like bats.
Laughter echoes loud, as the branches all sway,
A picnic of giggles starts every day.

With acorns as confetti and leaves all around,
The creatures make music, a whimsical sound.
The owls play the drums, and the foxes sing clear,
Every critter joins in, full of festive cheer.

Woodland Riddles

What did the tree say to the butterfly?
"Stop flitting around, just rest and don't fly!"
A riddle of nature, all giggles and play,
As the woodpecker knocks, in its own funny way.

The hedgehog tells tales that will make you all grin,
While the mushrooms just chuckle, with their silly spin.
A rabbit hops close, with a pun on the side,
In this curious glade where the humor won't hide.

The Tale of Twisting Trails

Once on a trail where the shadows all danced,
A turtle named Ted found his pocket had chanced.
He pulled out a snack, but it rolled down a hill,
Chased by a raccoon with a most lively thrill.

The path twisted round, like a giggle on grass,
The fox was quite clever, he'd run and he'd sass.
As the sun dipped low, they played tag in the dark,
Each corner a surprise, like a whimsical lark.

Serenity Under the Old Canopy

Under the leaves where the shadows do twist,
A frog in a tux begins to insist.
"Please join me for tea, it's a party to share!"
With laughter resounding, the forest’s affair.

The badgers bring cookies, the birds sing a tune,
While the old tree chuckles, beneath the bright moon.
With a sprinkle of joy and a dash of delight,
They dance until dawn, in the soft morning light.

Shadows Dance in Autumn Light

In autumn's glow, the leaves do sway,
A squirrel dances, come join the play.
With acorns flying, a joyful spree,
Who knew tree tops held such glee?

With branches tickling the sky so high,
A bird does croon, oh me, oh my!
The shadows waltz and play peek-a-boo,
As nature giggles, as if it knew.

Tales of Timber and Time

Old oak tells jokes, as wise as can be,
While a beaver chuckles, it gnaws with glee.
The roots share whispers of days long past,
While ants barter tales, oh how they amassed!

Each ring in the bark hides secrets galore,
As chipmunks trade stories of food and more.
The forest's a stage, with laughter in air,
Where trees play comedians, beyond compare.

The Spell of Sunlit Serenity

In dappled light where sunbeams hop,
A rabbit sings and does a flip-flop.
The windschime giggles, a tickle of breeze,
As flowers wear hats with such style and ease.

Butterflies flutter, with wings filled with flair,
While ants hold a circus right over there.
Even the shadows partake in the fun,
As laughter sparkles like bright morning sun.

Fables from the Forest Floor

On the forest floor, old tales unfold,
As mushrooms gossip, both daring and bold.
The snails tell stories while taking a snooze,
Of wild adventures and favorite views.

With ferns as the audience, all ears and green,
A fox cracks a joke, a real woodland scene.
Who knew the forest was such a delight?
Filled with humor and joy, both day and night.

Beneath Branches

Squirrels host a dance so bright,
With acorn hats, they twirl with might.
Branches bounce to the tune,
While birds chirp 'We're here till noon!'

A raccoon steals the show, quite sly,
He’s got his friends, oh my, oh my!
They juggle nuts, they laugh and play,
The forest is their grand café.

Beneath Stars

Under stars that wink and blink,
Fireflies join in, we’ll all sync.
An owl calls, 'Whooo's got the snacks?'
While chipmunks dance, no time to relax!

Those twinkling lights, a festive cheer,
Makes raccoon giggles, quite sincere.
With froggy jump and crickets’ song,
The night is fun, we all belong!

Sapling Serenades

Saplings sway with breezy tunes,
They hum their songs beneath the moon.
A little fox, wearing a crown,
Crash, bang, boom! The show's in town!

With wiggle-waggle and lots of spins,
They serenade the moonlit sins.
Dancing roots, they tap and slide,
While giggly leaves swirl in pride.

Twilight Tales of the Grove

Twilight whispers, secrets stray,
As fireflies giggle, 'Come and play!'
Raccoons tell tales of snacks galore,
While owls hoot, 'There’s always more!'

The breeze carries laughter far and wide,
With tree-hugging squirrels taking pride.
In shadows deep, fun never stops,
As laughter echoes through the treetops.

The Wonder of Woven Branches

Branches weave a tapestry grand,
Where critters prance, and friendships stand.
A hedgehog laughs, 'I lost my way!'
But finds a worm who joins the play.

With tangled vines, they spin around,
Creating joy where fun is found.
In every nook and twisty bend,
The forest is where smiles never end!

Underneath the Wooded Spell

Underneath the leafy crown,
A squirrel wears a tiny gown.
He dances with a nut so grand,
While birds form bands and take a stand.

A raccoon juggles acorns bright,
As fireflies twinkle through the night.
The rabbits laugh in playful cheer,
For mischief blooms when friends are near.

Gnomes in boots run all around,
While frogs go crazy with their sound.
With every whistle, hoot, and howl,
The forest bursts in laughter's prowl.

When the Forest Speaks

When the trees begin to chat,
A wise old owl wears a hat.
The trunks tell tales of cheeky sprites,
While mushrooms giggle, full of bites.

A bear who thinks he's quite the sage,
Recites his poems on a stage.
The bushes shake with wild delight,
As daisies dance beneath the light.

With whispers soft and secrets bold,
The forest shares its tales of old.
Each creature's voice, a silly song,
Together they sing all day long.

Enchanted Shelter

In a nook where shadows play,
A hedgehog hosts a cabaret.
With ants who waltz on tiny feet,
While crickets tap a groovy beat.

The foxes plot a midnight feast,
As their laughter does not cease.
Each twig and leaf becomes a stage,
For revelers, both young and sage.

A toadstool serves as courtly throne,
Where fairies gossip, never alone.
Beneath the branches, all is bright,
In this silly, starry night.

Lullabies of the Leafy Fortress

In the cradle of tangled vines,
The slumbering critters make their designs.
Bunnies snore in cozy piles,
As whispers drift through leafy aisles.

A sleepy owl hums a tune,
Under the watchful, grinning moon.
The nightingale croons to the crowd,
And every laugh rings pure and loud.

Mice compose sweet melodies,
Carried on the gentle breeze.
In the fortress made of green,
Dreams unfold where fun's routine.

Echoes of Ancient Boughs

In shadows where the squirrels play,
Old branches whisper jokes all day.
With acorns flying, laughter flows,
As woodland critters strike a pose.

A raccoon juggles, what a sight!
With every toss, he takes to flight.
The owls hoot in a wise dispute,
While chipmunks dance in furry suits.

If trees could chuckle, oh what joy,
They'd giggle at each prankster's ploy.
A leaf slides down with a swoosh and flap,
And lands smack-dab in a sleepy nap.

So come, dear friends, let's take a chance,
Join in the woodland's silly dance.
Amongst the boughs, let laughter ring,
For nature's joy is a funny thing!

Mysteries Wrapped in Green

Beneath each leaf, a riddle hides,
As woodland creatures pull their pranks with pride.
The owls wear glasses, wise and bright,
While bunnies plot a cake-filled night.

A fox plays tricks with a sneaky grin,
As sneaky as a shadow, almost akin.
The trees all chuckle, rustling their leaves,
While mushrooms giggle, “Oh, please! Oh, please!”

Skunks in suits wear bow ties so grand,
Hosting a banquet for the whole woodland band.
With each funny tale and cookie crumb,
The forest hums a joyous thrum.

From twinkling stars to the morning dew,
Secrets abound in every hue.
Join the dance 'neath the leafy arch,
To find the fun in this woodland march!

Celestial Glades and Woodland Whispers

In glades where sunbeams play and glide,
The mushrooms wiggle as beetles slide.
A gnome with jokes and a pointy hat,
Tells tales of giant, laughing cats.

The whispers weave through branches high,
As misty tales of clouds fly by.
A butterfly flutters, giggling in flight,
Tickling the flowers, oh what a sight!

The crickets croon in a comical tune,
While frogs debate who sings the best croon.
An acorn rolls with a splashy thud,
To join the party, splattering mud!

Under the stars, the night takes hold,
With stories of antics from the brave and bold.
Join in the revelry, it's quite absurd,
For nature's humor is rarely heard!

Harmony in the Heartwood

Deep in the woods where laughter grows,
The trees hold secrets which nobody knows.
A hedgehog in shades does a funky jig,
While snails in slippers groove big and big.

The rhymes of the forest are playful, indeed,
With laughter sprouting from every seed.
The raccoons debate who stole the pie,
While squirrels plot schemes as time flits by.

With every breeze comes a chuckling sound,
As pine cones drop with a comical bound.
A ticklish breeze ruffles each feathered friend,
Creating a symphony that won't ever end.

So gather 'round for a whimsical spree,
To join in the fun beneath each tree.
For joy is the rhythm in this silly wood,
And every critter is feeling good!

Serendipity Beneath the Green Canopy

Beneath the leaves, a squirrel prances,
In a tiny hat, it takes its chances.
Mice in tuxedos, they waltz here too,
While frogs in bow ties sing, ‘Who’s who?’

A picnic spread with crumbs of delight,
Ants in a conga line, what a sight!
A raccoon’s sneaking fries from a plate,
All join the dance, it just can’t wait!

The Magic Within the Grove

In a grove where gnomes wear red and blue,
They spin in circles, oh, what a view!
A chipmunk DJ plays beats so sweet,
While owls compete in a dance-off feat.

Hats made of leaves on every head,
Dancing and laughing, not a word said.
The moon peeks in, gives a cheeky grin,
'This party's wild; let the fun begin!'

Nightfall's Embrace

As shadows stretch, the stars all giggle,
A glow-worm flickers, what a wiggle!
A hedgehog hosting a late-night show,
With jokes about porcupines — oh, so slow!

Fireflies glow, wearing their best suits,
Telling tall tales of odd, tiny flukes.
The crickets chirp, their rhythmic delight,
While the moon yawns wide, ‘Is it morning yet?’

Where Shadows Dance with Silhouettes

Under the boughs where shadows play,
Laughter erupts, brightening the gray.
A raccoon spins in a silly twirl,
While a sleepy cat takes its lazy whirl.

The grass giggles when stepped upon,
Bouncing back like a cheerful brawn.
In the moon's glow, all are carefree,
Creating a world, just you and me!

Stars Within the Green Whisper

In the branches up high, a squirrel took flight,
He donned a small cape, on a whimsical night.
With acorns for jewels and a bark-covered throne,
He ruled over shadows, never feeling alone.

A chorus of crickets all gathered and played,
While chipmunks were dancing, unafraid of the fade.
They twirled and they spun, in the moon's glowing beam,
Creating a melody, like a sweet, silly dream.

The fireflies twinkled, a disco gone wild,
As raccoons collected, each mischief-filled child.
Each laugh in the dark made the night feel so bright,
In the land of green whispers, where fun takes to flight.

The Enchanted Canopy of Wandering Souls

A committee of owls held a meeting at dawn,
To argue and bicker, as wisdom was drawn.
With spectacles perched, they debated all night,
About who chased moonbeams and who flew just right.

A rabbit was late, with his fluffy formation,
Claiming that he'd lost all the sense of direction.
The trees rolled their branches, a rustling laugh,
As the bunny recounted his whimsical path.

Then came the wise fox with a riddle to share,
'Why do squirrels always seem to dance without care?'
The answer, he chuckled, and flipped on his tail,
'It's simply for joy, as their nuts never fail!'

Tales of Heartwood and Hushed Enchantment.

Underneath the wild leaves, a party awoke,
With raccoons and hedgehogs, each ready to poke.
They juggled bright mushrooms, tossed snacks in the air,
While a wise old tortoise declared it a fair.

In the quiet of twilight, a prankster appeared,
A fox in a cloak, trying hard to be feared.
But laughter erupted, his ruse fell apart,
With friends all around him, he stole the night's heart.

As shadows grew longer, the fun never ceased,
Each tale woven slowly, a laughter-filled feast.
With light in their eyes and joy in their shout,
Those heartwood tales whispered, 'There's no need to pout!'

Whispers of the Woodland

The trees turned to gossip, sharing secrets so bright,
About who wore what and who danced through the night.

A badger in boots? Oh, please, that's absurd!
But the crow shot back, 'Have you seen what I've heard?'

So, under the moonlight, each creature conspired,
To plan a wild fest, as the moonbeams conspired.
The toad in a hat croaked a tune so divine,
While snails in their shells formed a conga line.

With the laughter of leaves and the rustling of ferns,
The woodland was rumbling, with magic and turns.
For in the bright chaos, joy couldn't be tamed,
A funny little life in the forest proclaimed!

Spellbound Beneath Canopies of Time

In the glade where shadows play,
The squirrels dance in their own way.
With acorns thrown, they start a spree,
A waltz that's fuzzy as can be!

The branches creak, they clap their hands,
While birds in fancy outfits stand.
A picnic feast of crumbs and glee,
I swear I saw a dancing bee!

Whispers rustle in the breeze,
They tell me all the tree-folk tease.
With gossip ripe, they share their dreams,
And split their sides with silly schemes!

The roots below, they giggle too,
With every tickle, laugh ensues.
Here beneath the leafy dome,
I find my heart, I feel at home!

The Hidden Gem of Celestial Whispers

A toadstool sings a tune of cheer,
With mushroom hats, the party's near.
The ladybugs boast tales so tall,
While crickets chirp and hear it all.

The moonlight dances on the ground,
The fireflies buzz with a vibrant sound.
Each hidden gem, each twinkling light,
Makes merry spirits take their flight!

With twigs that tickle, she's a tease,
A breeze that swirls like soft cheese.
To lizards laughing in the shade,
Their slippery tricks will never fade!

The stars gather like glittering friends,
To join the fun as daylight ends.
With laughter ringing through the night,
The hidden gem shines oh-so-bright!

Journeys into the Heartwood Mystique

Through the brambles and thorns we go,
In search of giggles and a friendly crow.
We stumble on roots that tie us tight,
Yelling, 'Hey, this feels just right!'

Branches reach out with a swish and a sway,
Calling us forth to join in play.
Each step a riddle, oh what a jest,
This heartwood hides the very best!

Frogs in top hats croak the news,
While butterflies don their fanciest shoes.
We'll loop and twirl, in dizzy delight,
As the heartwood spins us through the night!

With every giggle, we chase the sun,
In this age-old game of fun!
Journeys here will never cease,
In heartwood's hug, we find our peace!

Echoes of Enchantment in Foliage

Underneath the leafy peak,
Chirps and chortles we all seek.
With playful vines that twist and tug,
A squirrel waves, a cheery shrug!

The rustling leaves begin to hum,
A silly song, oh what fun!
Bouncing beetles join the song,
Surrounded by friends, we can’t go wrong!

In the laughter of the trees,
We find our wishes on the breeze.
With sunbeams framing our delight,
Emerald whispers through the night!

Each echo brings a silly grin,
In this wild woodland, we all win.
So come along, let’s play and sing,
In enchanted leaves, we crown the spring!

Sylvan Echoes of Forgotten Lore

In a forest where squirrels wear hats,
A wise old owl gives out free spats.
Raccoons juggle acorns with flair,
While rabbits proclaim, "We just don't care!"

The trees whisper secrets, oh so bold,
Telling tales from ages old.
A fox dons a monocle, looking quite grand,
And dances on branches, oh isn't it grand?

With mushrooms like umbrellas, they gossip and jest,
The critters host parties, oh what a fest!
They'll tell you of lost socks and missing shoes,
As they sip on dew drops and share the news.

So if you tread softly, you might catch a sight,
Of merry woodland creatures dancing at night.
In this realm of whimsy, laughter fills the air,
For in this green kingdom, no worry nor care.

The Spellbinding Shade of Serenity

Under the spread of a grand old oak,
A family of chipmunks share jokes and smoke.
A snail claims he's the fastest on track,
While the turtles just laugh, “We’ve got no lack!”

A breeze stirs the leaves, they giggle out loud,
As ants in tuxedos strut, feeling proud.
A shadowy raccoon sells lemonade cheap,
While squirrels crack jokes that make no sense leap.

With picnic blankets sprawled where the sun glows bright,

The thrumming of laughter makes everything right.
They spell out their secrets with sticks in the dirt,
For the trees hold their stories, never to hurt.

So come take a rest in this shaded domain,
Where giggles are plenty, and boredom’s a bane.
Join the woodland club, it’s a curious crew,
In the shade of great trees, there’s always a view.

Nestled Between Timeworn Trunks

Between the gnarled roots, something stirs,
A trail of small footprints, oh, who prefers?
A hedgehog on roller skates zooms with glee,
While an ant follows closely, as quick as can be!

Old branches bend low, like wise wiggly friends,
Sharing tall tales of the forest's good ends.
A frog leaps in rhythm, croaking lively tunes,
While ducks debate fashion and the light of the moons.

With giggles and grumbles, the sun starts to fade,
As shadows grow longer, avoiding their shade.
A crow caws for dinner, a feast of delight.
Where friends gather close, and share tales of fright.

So come to this nook, where fun seldom stops,
Join in the laughter as the daylight just tops.
For here in this haven, joy’s never far,
Between timeworn trunks, beneath the bright star.

Fables in the Lattice of Limbs

In the lattice of limbs, a story unfolds,
Where a jester of bears creates laughter of gold.
With juggling of berries, they toss in the air,
While a hedgehog looks on with a curious stare.

A parrot named Doodle sketches up dreams,
Tales of grand adventures and wild, wacky schemes.
With each flap of wings, a new tale's initiated,
As laughter erupts—never to be underrated!

A picnic of honey and berries galore,
Sipped with the warmth of sweet tales in store.
The rabbits debate who's the fastest of all,
While the wise turtle chuckles from under his crawl.

So gather your friends where stories run free,
In the lattice of limbs, join the happy spree.
With each woven fable, a new laugh appears,
Celebrating life through giggles and cheers.

Rooted Reveries

In a forest where squirrels wear hats,
And chipmunks have dance parties with bats.
A tree with a laugh, shakes its leafy crown,
While raccoons hold court, in their jester's gown.

A woodpecker's tap is a drummer's beat,
As ants in a line march, oh so discreet.
The sun spills its giggles, bouncing off the ground,
While butterflies swirl, in their polka-dot gown.

Old branches creak tales, both funny and bright,
Of owls who try jokes at the fall of night.
A deer drops a pun, and the bushes all shake,
With laughter that ripples, in each little lake.

Each root has a story, a joke to unfold,
Like the one of the tree, who thinks he's so bold.
He sways in the breeze, with a chuckle sincere,
“Come sit in my shade, let’s spread joy and cheer!”

The Quiet Beneath the Bark

Where whispers of leaves tickle the air,
The critters below hold a secret affair.
A turtle in tie, part of a grand act,
With an audience wrapped in their leafy pact.

The ants gossip tale of the snail who was late,
His shell had a joke, it just couldn't wait.
A hedgehog told riddles, beneath the cool gloom,
While beetles played cards in their glimmering room.

Frogs croak the news, with comedic flair,
About a lost shoe, that landed somewhere.
An owl winks slyly, with feathers so neat,
As tales of the wood pile bring laughter to feet.

So join in the laughter, the giggling spree,
Beneath this big giant, so cheerful and free.
For in every knot, and each gnarled mark,
Lies a tickle of joy, in the quiet and dark.

Nature's Covert Chants

In the heart of the woods where secrets sing,
A squirrel once tried to impersonate spring.
With flowers on his head, he danced on a log,
While frogs croaked their laughter, mistaking him a fog.

A wise old raccoon with dreams of donut
Held meetings at night, where all critters would run.
They plotted and planned, each quite a character,
Beneath the soft glow, each hidden plan’s factor.

The owls wore glasses, but could never see right,
They pondered deep thoughts, then took off in flight.
A bee organized buzz, all around in a whirl,
Spread tales of a pie made by a wandering girl.

In this realm of the quirky, the trees seem to smirk,
Their branches nod knowingly, as shadows embark.
For laughter is plenty, and joy’s never far,
In this clandestine place, that’s just who they are.

Dreams in the Thicket

In a thicket of dreams where the snickers grow,
A porcupine gabs, putting on quite a show.
With quills in a plume, he spins tales on a whim,
While hedgehogs applaud with a joyful grim.

Underneath the Emerald Enchantment

Beneath the boughs where squirrels play,
I told a joke that made them sway.
They giggled hard, the leaves did shake,
And one fell down—what a mistake!

The mushrooms laughed, a clever lot,
With tiny hats, they danced a lot.
A rabbit winked, a hedgehog spun,
In this green world, we all have fun!

The acorns rolled, a merry race,
While chipmunks joined with happy pace.
The sun peeked through, a smiling face—
Who knew they'd have such wild embrace?

So if you wander, take a seat,
In nature's laugh, there's joy so sweet.
Just watch your step, and mind your hat,
Or you'll be tangled in this chat!

Light and Leaf: A Gentle Kiss

A leaf fell down, a twirling fall,
And landed right on Bunny's ball.
He bounced it back with such a flair,
And split his ears, oh what a scare!

The sunlight giggled through the trees,
While owls hooted with swinging knees.
A breeze that whispered jokes and puns,
Made shadows dance, all just for fun!

The flowers danced in bright array,
While ants joined in a conga play.
They marched along, a tiny crew,
In colors bold, with vibrant hue.

So if you find a sunny glen,
Just stop and smile with all your friends.
For under leaves, where laughter grows,
The light and leaf bring comic woes!

The Forest's Veiled Symphony

In tangled limbs, the critters sing,
A symphony of everything.
With silly tunes on breezy nights,
They serenade the firefly lights.

The owls shout “Hoot!” in grand surprise,
While bees buzz round with tiny eyes.
A fox in shades serenades the morn,
With notes so sharp, it leaves them worn!

The trees must listen—what a show!
Their bark’s a laugh, in rhythmic flow.
The whispers soft, the branches sway,
A show for all, in nature's play.

So if you hear a forest song,
Join in the dance, you can’t be wrong!
With all its quirks and vibrant cheer,
Under the stars, you’ll find your peer!

Ciphers of the Canopy

A secret code in leaves so green,
Causing giggles, oh what a scene!
The whispers rustle, branches tease,
As critters scurry with great ease.

The squirrels play the acorn game,
With bets on nuts, oh what a fame!
The rabbits hop, they've cracked the code,
As hedgehogs cheer, lighting the road.

Beneath the vines, they crack a laugh,
With riddles spun, in nature's craft.
The shadows twitch, the dance goes on,
In this green world, we laugh till dawn!

So join the crew, twist like the vines,
For all your chuckles, the tree outlines.
In ciphers whispered, joy will sprout,
Beneath the green, there's no doubt!

Chronicles of the Burrowed Enchantment

In a hollow so deep, where the critters convene,
There's a squirrel in a jacket, looking rather keen.
He flips pancakes high, with a flick of his tail,
While a hedgehog named Chuck weighs the syrup in scale.

A rabbit on skates races round in a blur,
Juggling acorns and nuts, making quite the stir.
A wise owl in glasses shouts, "Don’t drop your pie!"
While the ants start a band, with a sax and a fry.

Under roots that are thick, stories twist and twine,
Frogs tell of a party with noodles and wine.
But the punch bowl got stolen, oh what a mishap,
It turned out a fox, wearing a fancy cap!

They all gather ‘round, sharing giggles and glee,
In a burrow so snug, where nothing's quite free.
So if you hear laughter, just peek with delight,
There’s a world full of wonders, lit up by moonlight.

Whimsy Woven in Sap and Shadow

In the shadiest nook, where the shadows do dance,
A raccoon named Percy invented romance.
With a hat made of leaves, and a bowtie of bark,
He serenades crickets, all through till it's dark.

A snail with a top hat glides down from the trees,
Reciting bad jokes with impeccable ease.
But the jokes get so twisted, they tumble and fall,
As the audience rolls, laughing one and all.

On a stage made of mushrooms, the beetles all sing,
While the fireflies flicker, providing a fling.
Tadpoles bring harmony, croaking in tune,
For the grand silliness that ends far too soon.

So if you should wander, and hear all the cheer,
Just follow the laughter, it's waiting right here.
There's a place in the woods, where the silly unite,
And the joy keeps on growing, all day and all night!

The Glade where Wishes Take Flight

In a glade filled with wishes, the butterflies roam,
A bear named Paul Prancer considers a home.
He dreams of a sofa made soft with a quilt,
But tripped on a rock, fell over the silt.

The rabbits all gather with popcorn in hand,
As a goat tells tall tales, they can barely withstand.
They laugh and they giggle, until they turn red,
And the wise old badger just shakes his big head.

There’s a tree that has secrets, it whispers and sighs,
About fish that wear hats and ducks in disguise.
And somewhere a cat plays a tune on a flute,
While doing a dance in a bright polka suit.

In this glade full of laughter, where dreams drift and twirl,
Every moment brings joy, every spin makes you whirl.
So next time you wander, where the wild things ignite,
Just remember it’s silly, and wishes take flight!

Secrets of the Serene Sanctuary

In a calm little nook, where the sunlight does peek,
Lives a turtle named Timmy who's shabby but sleek.
He wears a loud bowtie, quite the colorful sight,
As he races on foot, with a sloth in the night.

The fireflies giggle, lighting paths with a glow,
While a lizard named Larry performs for the show.
He juggles some jellybeans, then slips with a yelp,
Causing everyone there to just crack up and help.

With the crickets on drums, and the spiders in suits,
The party just buzzes, while dancing in boots.
There's a rumor that somewhere, a cake's running wild,
But they giggle and laugh—'twas a curious child.

In the serene little refuge where silliness reigns,
The critters all gather, ignoring the pains.
So next time you wander through branches and dew,
Don't forget to stop by, and join in the crew!

The Leafy Labyrinth

In a maze of green, squirrels play,
They'll steal your snack, then scamper away.
Leaves whisper secrets, oh so sly,
While a puzzled rabbit hops by and sighs.

The paths twist and turn with a giggle,
Where shadows dance and sunlight wiggles.
A lost child shouts, 'Where's the way out?'
A wise old turtle grins, 'No need to pout!'

Beneath the branches, laughter spills,
As ants form a parade, ignoring the thrills.
With acorns as crowns, they'd strut and preen,
In this leafy maze, the fun's evergreen.

So if you get lost, don't shed any tears,
Join the fun with the critters that cheer.
For in the labyrinth, you'll find the key,
Just laugh a little, and you'll be free!

Stories of the Sylvan Realm

Underneath the branches wide,
There’s a tale where the forest hides.
A fox read books with oversized specs,
While deep in thought, he puzzled the hex.

The owls hoot riddles, wise and old,
While the chipmunks giggle, their antics bold.
Acorns roll, and the laughter flows,
As stories twist in the mischievous prose.

Dancing in circles, the butterflies prance,
Making the flowers sway in their dance.
A grumpy old bear drops his honey pot,
And suddenly, hilarity's caught!

The trees are ears to the joyous sound,
As foolish tales echo all around.
In the sylvan realm, where silliness beams,
Each leaf holds a story, spun from dreams.

Charms of the Forest's Embrace

The trees wear cloaks made of mossy green,
In their embrace, a charming scene.
The raccoons plan a late-night feast,\nWhile the owls hoot, 'You’re all out at least!'

A playful breeze tickles the leaves,
Whispering secrets, what fun it weaves!
A frog in a top hat leaps with delight,
Inviting all critters for a grand night.

With shadows waltzing, and fireflies glow,
The woodland creatures put on a show.
A hedgehog juggles with acorns round,
As laughter and cheers echo all around.

So join the dance in this cozy space,
With giggles and joy in the forest's embrace.
In a world where whimsy finds its place,
The charms of the woods always leave a trace.

Pinecone Prose

Once a pinecone wanted to fly,
With dreams so big, it reached for the sky.
'Toss me high!' it cried, in a leafy plea,
But ended up snug in a bumblebee's spree.

Laughing so hard, the trees shook with glee,
As the pinecone spun around, so carefree.
The bees buzzed back, 'You can’t be a bird!'
But pinecone just giggled, unfazed by the word.

With acorn friends, it plotted a show,
To win over skies, and steal the glow.
They built a rocket out of twigs and leaves,
But launched too soon, what a sight, oh please!

Crash in the bushes, laughter all around,
Pinecone just chuckled, lost and found.
In the forest's heart, with fate so fine,
Even a pinecone can dream and shine.

Murmurs Among the Moss

Underneath the leafy crown,
A squirrel wears a tiny frown.
His acorn stash has gone astray,
He blames the birds for flying away.

The moss whispers to passing bugs,
‘Hey, have you seen his missing jugs?’
They laugh and dance, the cheeky crew,
While the squirrel plots a comeback too.

Laughter spills from twisted roots,
As ants march in their silly suits.
The woodland’s stage, a comedy,
Where tree trunks nod, 'Oh, look at he!'

With giggles drifting on the breeze,
Nature’s jesters, aiming to please.
Under the tree, joy’s always free,
As nature’s pranksters playfully flee.

The Serenity of Shaded Moments

In the shade where giggles bloom,
A raccoon dances, shaking his room.
His tail a feather, oh so grand,
He scrounges snacks with an expert hand.

The breeze tickles, whispers low,
While chipmunks put on a show.
With acorns tossed in a fun pursuit,
Who knew nature was so astute?

A shadowy seat for pretty naps,
Where sunlight sips from leafy laps.
Laughter echoes, a silly song,
As nature's clowns join in the throng.

Each shaded moment full of cheer,
Bring on the giggles, bring them here!
For life beneath the branches bright,
Is filled with fun, pure delight.

Tapestry of Branches and Breezes

Within the branches, wise and old,
A worm spins tales, daring and bold.
He whispers secrets in the wind,
While birds roll eyes and laugh, transfixed.

The leaves shake hands with the wandering breeze,
While raccoons giggle, ‘Oh, what a tease!’
“Is it a tree or a clown’s hat?”
Scribbles of laughter, stitched, just like that!

Sunbeams waltz, a bright parade,
While spiders weave their funny charade.
They dance on strings like tiny stars,
Sipping dew from their high-up bars.

A tapestry spun from leafy yarn,
Frolicking shadows, the bunny's charm.
Each twist and turn, a giggle’s trace,
Under the branches, a whimsical place.

Secrets of Seasons Past

Leaves chat softly of days gone by,
When winter's chill made the crickets sigh.
A parade of flakes with fuzzy hats,
And squirrels skate while wearing spats.

In autumn's glow, they tell the tales,
Of pumpkins dancing on gusty gales.
Nuts rolling like tiny trucks,
While hedgehogs giggle, just for kicks.

Wandering whispers of spring's grand schemes,
Flowers chuckling at nature's dreams.
Each petal ruffled, a whimsical call,
As bees humorously bumble and sprawl.

So gather 'round, oh curious folk,
For life's a jest, and love's the joke.
In the shade, where chortles bloom,
Every secret grows with room for room.

Moonlit Murmurs of Woodland Spirits

In shadows deep, the critters play,
A raccoon juggles, night turns to day.
Squirrels dance with a silly flair,
While owls hoot puns that float in the air.

Beneath the stars, the frogs croak tunes,
While fireflies blink like tiny balloons.
A rabbit spins tales of his last meal,
With every jump, he twirls like a wheel.

Wise old trees lean in to hear,
The gossip of creatures, absurd yet dear.
A badger whispers jokes that stick,
As the night rolls on, and time starts to tick.

Laughter echoes through the night,
With every prank, joy feels just right.
In this woodland realm so full of cheer,
The spirits of fun come dancing near.

Beneath the Canopy of Wonder

Beneath the leaves, where shadows lurk,
A hedgehog sighs, his back in the dirt.
He says, 'Do you think I look like a hat?
I'm quite the fashionista, imagine that!'

A squirrel spins tales, all grand and bold,
Of acorns he found when the weather was cold.
'They wear tiny boots!' he claims with a laugh,
While chipmunks giggle, sharing the gaffe.

Nearby, a turtle with a slow-motion grin,
Recites a poem, hoping to win.
His words, though slow, eventually rhyme,
And soon the whole forest chimes in on time.

With each silly story, the woods come alive,
Where laughter and whimsy lead the drive.
So gather round, all, with joy that's true,
For under the branches, the fun's just for you.

A Reverie Among the Gnarled Branches

Among the branches, the shadows play,
A wise old owl gives quizzes all day.
'Which came first, the chicken or egg?'
The answer he gives, makes everyone beg.

A mischievous fox shares his secret stash,
Of mushrooms that glow in a purple flash.
With a wink and a grin, he bars the gate,
'Only for friends, or it might be too late!'

The trees stand tall with trunks so wide,
In their knotted arms, all dreams can hide.
Squirrels debate the best type of nut,
While a raccoon eavesdrops, lurking in a rut.

Each gnarled branch sings a lullaby,
To creatures that scamper beneath the sky.
With laughter, they weave a tapestry bright,
In this whimsical realm, hearts take flight.

Timeless Tales in the Forest's Heart

In the forest's heart, where laughter rings,
A rabbit recites the dumbest of things.
'What do you call a bear with no teeth?
A gummy bear!' brings joy to the heath.

A wise-cracking crow shares jokes on a wire,
While chipmunks dance, never seem to tire.
'There's a party tonight, don’t be late!'
Squeaks a chipmunk, as the sun starts to fade.

Trees sway along with a rhythm so grand,
Encouraging all for a woodland band.
They play with sticks, leaves flutter and twirl,
As the forest fills with a whimsical swirl.

And as the night falls, with stars in sight,
They gather 'round, it's a pure delight.
With tales that twist and laughter that flows,
In this timeless world, everyone knows.

Enchanted Explorations Below

Beneath the branches, shadows creep,
Squirrels chatter, secrets to keep.
Gnomes in hats, they dance and twirl,
Spilling acorns, what a whirl!

A rabbit hops with shoes so fine,
Telling tales over berry wine.
The mushrooms laugh, a giggly crew,
Who knew fungi could wear a shoe?

A raccoon juggles shiny finds,
While owls hoot their clever lines.
Every nook, a treasure trove,
In this land where giggles rove!

So take a seat on mossy ground,
Let laughter echo all around.
Who knew under leaves' dense cover,
Lay worlds of fun with friends to discover?

Secrets in the Shadows

A whispered joke, the pines agree,
As chipmunks snicker, full of glee.
A shadowy figure, what could it be?
Oh dear, it's just a bumblebee!

The branches sway, the leaves confide,
Spooky stories that squirrels provide.
A fox with glasses reads the news,
Oh my, the headlines? Just silly views!

Talkative frogs croak a tune,
Their chorus perfect under the moon.
A hedgehog plays the jazz trombone,
While a turtle tries to find his phone!

In this grove, where whispers ring,
The funny tales are bubbling spring.
Join the party, lose your frown,
Find the hilarity in the brown!

Echo Chamber of the Ancients

In hollow trunks, old tales abound,
Echoes of laughter, a joyful sound.
Tree spirits chuckle at human plight,
As owls roll their eyes, their wings take flight!

A wise old tortoise loses the race,
While squirrels tease, in a speedy chase.
A raccoon wearing socks played a trick,
He stole the spoons with a sly little flick!

Napping critters wake with a start,
As whispers tickle their furry heart.
Leafy confetti, a whimsical shower,
Cascades down from an ancient tower!

Each echo carries a jest from the past,
Grins from the roots hold stories vast.
Join the fun, let your worries cease,
In this woodland where laughter's the lease!

Dreamscapes of the Shady Refuge

Under the boughs, a dream takes flight,
Bunnies in pajamas dance through the night.
A sleepwalking fox heads to a feast,
Stumbling on mushrooms, not one, but least!

A turtle spins tales that twist and twirl,
While fireflies waltz in a glowing whirl.
The whispers of leaves are a playful tease,
As dragonflies giggle with the greatest ease!

A picnic blanket full of snacks,
Gathering critters to share some laughs.
Peanut butter sandwiches with jam so sticky,
And pudding cups that are rather tricky!

In this refuge where dreamers play,
Mirthful moments brighten the day.
Take a nap, join the funny parade,
In this sleepy glen where joy won't fade!

Whirling Leaves of Lore

In autumn's grasp, they spin and glide,
A dance of leaves where squirrels hide.
With acorns flying, giggles rise,
A nutty feast beneath blue skies.

The breeze it chuckles, branches bend,
As nature's pranks begin to send.
A joyful riot, a leafy chase,
A tumble here, a merry race.

With every gust, a caper's birth,
A twirling show upon the earth.
Among the trunks, a hidden stash,
Of playful sprites who leave in a flash!

So let us whirl, in leaf and cheer,
With nature's boon, there's naught to fear.
In every breeze, a jest displayed,
In whirling leaves, our laughter played.

Beneath the Whispering Willows

The willows sway with tales to tell,
Of frogs in suits and fish that yell.
With every rustle, secrets spill,
Of gnome-sized parties on the hill.

A cat shows up, a hat on head,
Proclaiming all who dare to tread.
He speaks in riddles, laughs a lot,
While dancing 'round the garden pot.

Squirrels wear coats, and owls give clues,
In this wild world, we can't refuse.
A ruckus here, a giggle there,
In whispers low, we all must share.

So come, my friend, let’s roam and play,
Where willows speak in a jesting way.
In nature's whimsy, we shall find,
A hilarious joy that’s truly kind.

Echoes of the Emerald Grove

In emerald gowns, the trees convene,
With branches swaying, none too lean.
They share their jokes, the bark it creaks,
While sunlight streams and the forest speaks.

A rabbit hops, a funny sight,
With floppy ears, it takes to flight.
It bounces high, it trips and rolls,
In laughter loud, it spills its soul.

The songbirds chirp their silly tunes,
Challenging the light of moons.
With every note, a chuckle flies,
While leaves above join in the highs.

Oh, come and sit among the green,
Where fun and folly reign supreme.
In echoes bright, we'll find our way,
In the grove's embrace, let's laugh and play.

Ethereal Shadows at Dusk

As twilight falls with gentle grace,
The shadows dance, take up their space.
With laughs that bubble, spirits rise,
As night unveils its playful guise.

The fox in socks prances around,
A jester lost, but joy is found.
With glittering eyes, it twirls and spins,
Inviting all to join the whims.

The crickets play a lively beat,
As fireflies twinkle, never discreet.
An evening feast of jokes and tricks,
In the twilight hour, our laughter clicks.

So here we stand, with friend and cheer,
In phantom play, let's persevere.
With every chuckle, dusk takes flight,
In ethereal shadows, hearts feel light.

Reveries Wrapped in Roots

Beneath the giggling branches wide,
Squirrels whisper secrets, side by side.
The toadstools dance with grace and flair,
While ants parade in their tiny lair.

A rabbit tickles a sleepy fox,
As trees start wearing mismatched socks.
The breeze throws confetti from the sky,
And rabbits giggle as they hop by.

Old wise owl tells tales of delight,
How a snail outran a mouse in flight.
With acorns rolling like marbles below,
The forest laughs at every show.

In this realm where whimsy reigns,
Even the shadows play silly games.
With each rustle, the laughter grows,
As critters wiggle their tiny toes.

Heartbeats of the Earth

From roots arise giggles loud and clear,
As beetles roller skate faster than cheer.
Worms in tuxedos wiggle in style,
While gnarled trees grin all the while.

The ground is alive with a merry tune,
As mushrooms hop under the bright full moon.
With laughter echoing through leafy halls,
The flowers sway, giggling in thralls.

A critter chef flips pancakes quite high,
While bees buzzing softly hum lullabies.
The earth chuckles with every beat,
Making sure our hearts feel the heat.

Juggling stones, the children of soil,
Create a ruckus, never to foil.
In this wonderland, joy takes its seed,
As nature's pulse plants every need.

The Spellbound Sylvan Glade

In a grove where jesters always play,
And shadows skip through twilight's sway.
A wooden frog croaks riddles so wide,
While fireflies twinkle, like stars that glide.

The grass tickles toes as we dance around,
While squirrels on stilts jump off the ground.
With giggles and snorts, the mushrooms cheer,
For every clumsy fall brings more to dear.

The breeze sings high with a twirling tune,
As owls hoot softly, “It’s afternoon!”
With mice wearing hats made of fallen pine,
Life’s a circus, everything’s just fine.

A parade of petals goes swirling by,
The trees wave their branches, oh my, oh my!
Laughter spills out from bark and from bough,
This enchanted spot takes an endless bow.

Soft Light Through Fallen Leaves

Light dances playfully on the ground,
As critters in huddles create merry sound.
A hedgehog hiccups, a chipmunk sings,
In this world, joy tugs at your strings.

The leaves whisper secrets of laughter and glee,
As shadows paint stories, just come and see!
With dandelion wishes that flutter and sway,
Time ticks in tickles, come laugh and play.

Frogs tell jokes while balancing stones,
While squirrels mime out their silly tones.
The sun peeks through like a giggling friend,
Where whimsy and smiles just never end.

In glimmers of gold and soft, playful glow,
Nature’s exuberance steals quite the show.
Join the fiesta, don’t miss the fun,
Beneath the warm light of the cheerful sun.

The Enigma of Canopied Stars

In a forest so thick, with wonders galore,
Squirrels debate, who can climb more?
They jump and they frolic, oh what a sight,
Creating their own circus, day and night.

A raccoon with a hat steals a shoe,
Contemplating styles, it's absurd but true!
The trees chuckle softly as leaves start to sway,
Wondering which critter will dance the best ballet.

Owls take bets on who'll get the next treat,
Sipping on dew drops, they think it's sweet.
While twisty old branches form a jury,
Awaiting a verdict of furry or blurry.

As the sun dips low and the laughter grows bright,
The forest prepares for a wild, starry night.
With all their antics, they're never alone,
In this whimsical world, their joy has grown.

Nature's Hidden Alchemy

Mushrooms wear hats, like fanciful cheer,
Whispering secrets only squirrels can hear.
Frogs in tuxedos hop by the stream,
Planning a gala—a quirky daydream.

Weeds throw a party that nobody knows,
With dandelions spinning in whimsical clothes.
The earthworms are dancing, all covered in grime,
Judging the beetles on their rhythm and rhyme.

Ants on parade, quite the sight to behold,
Selling lemonade made from flowers of gold.
The trees give advice, with a nod and a grin,
As the critters create, let the fun begin!

Beneath the bright canopy, laughter resounds,
In this land of strange wonders where joy knows no bounds.
With laughter and mischief sparkling all around,
In this alchemy of nature, joy can be found.

Beneath the Verdant Veil of Silence

Shhh! Hear that giggle from the moss-covered rocks?
It’s a hedgehog playing dress-up, with shiny gold socks.
The shadows are dancing, with dust in the breeze,
While crickets hold concerts and hum their sweet keys.

Snakes wear their stripes like a fancy parade,
While lizards laugh loudly, unafraid.
Under arches of leaves, secrets are spun,
As fireflies twinkle, illuminating the fun.

A caterpillar twirls, showing off its new shoes,
But the butterflies giggle, wearing hues not to lose.
The flowers all nod, joining in on the jest,
In this hidden nook, nature’s humor is blessed.

When night falls, the laughter still lingers around,
With stars peeking down, the joy knows no bound.
In this playful theater, all creatures unite,
Underneath veils of silence, they dance through the night.

A Tapestry of Roots and Radiance

In a realm where roots are like little soft paws,
Digging for treasures, they've broken the laws.
With whispers of grass that tickle the air,
Every inch has a story, bursting with flair.

Fungi in pajamas gossip away,
While bugs wear bowties for a grand soirée.
The breeze sings ballads of past silly fights,
As branches hold secrets beneath silver lights.

Bouncing baby bunnies dip into a race,
With turtles on stilts, keeping up the pace.
Each twig celebrates with a jolly old cheer,
As the birdwatchers chuckle at their frenetic sphere.

Dancing beneath colors too vibrant to see,
The tapestry weaves what it means to be free.
Among roots and radiance, laughter ignites,
In this forest of fun, where whimsy delights.

Whispers of the Ancient Roots

Under branches, squirrels conspire,
Raccoons share tales of mischief and mire.
A gnome in the shadows, with a fez on his head,
Once chased a leaf, but fell out of bed.

The roots giggle softly, while critters all play,
A frog croaks a tune, trying to sway.
But the beetles bring chaos, and dance like a fool,
As ants whip up snacks, that's their golden rule.

With laughter that tickles the low hanging fruit,
A hedgehog spins stories, in a tiny red suit.
They gather 'round nightly for games and for feasts,
While fireflies blink, as the starry sky teasts.

So come join the fun, if you dare and you please,
But beware of the pinecones that might knock your knees!
For here in this realm, where the odd truly reigns,
Life's merry and silly, with giggles and gains.

Shadows Dance with Woven Dreams

Where shadows shiver and twirl in delight,
The fairies delight in a wild, crazy fight.
A chorus of crickets play tunes on the grass,
While a hedgehog slides by, with boots made of glass.

Leaves whisper secrets that tickle the night,
As a woodpecker hoots, joining in the flight.
The breeze becomes giggles, the moon starts to grin,
And a squirrel sets up for a grand party win!

They toss acorns like balls, with good spirits ablaze,
While shadows leap wildly in a comical haze.
The owls can't help but join in the show,
Bringing wisdom with laughter, the best way to grow.

So if you're feeling dull, or a bit in a funk,
Just dance with the shadows, and give them a skunk.
For here, under branches, fun thrives night and day,
With whimsy and laughter leading the way.

Enchanted Leaves in Twilight's Embrace

In the twilight's glow, where the giggles ignite,
Leaves rustle with secrets, in soft, fading light.
A raccoon with a hat tells tales of his heist,
While a gopher insists, “Don’t you dare throw rice!”

The frogs are all crooning some wild serenade,
As twirling vines whirl, in their leafy parade.
A shadow approaches with a skip and a hop,
It’s Timmy the turtle, ready to stop!

He’s got snacks on his back, like a backpack in style,
Says, “Join in the fun, just stay for a while!”
The laughter grows loud as the dusk starts to fade,
While a hedgehog juggles, in love with his trade.

So gather, dear friends, where the silly prevails,
In the garden of whimsy, where joy never pales.
We’ll dance with the night, ‘neath the starlit embrace,
And leave with a grin on our fun-loving face.

Secrets Nestled in Bark and Bough

In the cozy nooks where the creatures all hide,
Whispers twirl softly, like a feathered glide.
An owl wears cool glasses, with styles quite bizarre,
And a badger brings snacks from his oversized jar.

Fungi throw parties, with strobe lights aglow,
While worms sing sweet ballads, putting on a show.
The bees buzz along with the rhythm and beat,
Each secret unravels, as they dance on their feet.

Underneath all the laughter, a mystery brews,
As critters exchange their most whimsical views.
A cat in a top hat juggles stones made of cheese,
And everyone laughs, saying, “This is a tease!”

So come one, come all, take a seat on the grass,
For a night full of joy, where shenanigans pass.
With secrets a’ buzzing, wrapped in laughter’s embrace,
This forest of wonder, is a magical place.

Hushed Harmonies of Nature

In the shade, a squirrel prances,
Twisting through the merry branches.
Leaves giggle with every rustle,
Nature’s choir joins the hustle.

A frog wears a crown made of dew,
Croaking out his royal view.
Birds serenade with silly tweets,
While rabbits dance on tiny feet.

Whispers from the Woodland Realm

Underfoot, the acorns roll,
Whispering secrets, oh so droll.
Deer wear glasses, reading maps,
While foxes take their afternoon naps.

Mushrooms gossip, sharing tales,
Of woodland kings and silly jails.
Raccoons fashion hats from leaves,
Telling jokes to passers-by thieves.

Charms and Chimeras Amongst the Bark

Beneath the bark, a creature sleeps,
Dreaming of counting endless sheep.
A beaver builds a wobbly tower,
Declaring himself the building power.

Frogs play cards with the fireflies,
Betting glow upon the skies.
The chipmunks throw a grand parade,
As dragonflies serenade the glade.

The Forest's Heartfelt Secrets

In hidden nooks, the secrets grow,
Covered by a blanket of mossy flow.
A bear in pajamas takes his tea,
Laughing with BBQ in the breeze.

Owl wears glasses, wise as can be,
Winking at all with glee-filled decree.
At night, the stars play hide and seek,
While crickets chirp, oh so unique.

Milton Keynes UK
Ingram Content Group UK Ltd.
UKHW021241191124
451300UK00007B/172

9 789916 940921